Hannah B. Gage

**The Land by the Sunset Sea and other Poems**

Hannah B. Gage

**The Land by the Sunset Sea and other Poems**

ISBN/EAN: 9783743329058

Manufactured in Europe, USA, Canada, Australia, Japa

Cover: Foto ©ninafisch / pixelio.de

Manufactured and distributed by brebook publishing software (www.brebook.com)

Hannah B. Gage

**The Land by the Sunset Sea and other Poems**

## CONTENTS.

|  | PAGE |
|---|---|
| Proem, | 1 |
| The Land by the Sunset Sea, | 3 |
| Retrospection, | 8 |
| A Thought, | 11 |
| Two Views of Life, | 12 |
| The Happy Medium, | 14 |
| A Kiss, | 15 |
| A Picture, | 16 |
| The Kiss, | 17 |
| Only a Broken Rosebud, | 18 |
| Skating, | 20 |
| Written on the Fly-leaf of My Diary, | 21 |
| Unspoken Thoughts, | 23 |
| "Half-Mast," | 25 |
| A Face, | 27 |

|  | PAGE |
|---|---|
| Kisses, | 28 |
| Life, | 29 |
| A Friend in Need, | 31 |
| The Eagle, | 32 |
| James A. Garfield, | 33 |
| Nan, | 34 |
| Winding up Time, | 36 |
| Birdie, | 38 |
| Kris Kringle, | 39 |
| Christmas Eve, | 43 |
| Christmas, | 45 |
| New Year's Eve, | 47 |
| My Caller, | 49 |
| New Year's Callers, | 51 |
| Only Friends, | 54 |
| Waiting for Santa Claus, | 58 |
| Baby Wisdom, | 65 |
| 1979, | 66 |
| Retribution, | 73 |
| Jack Thornton's Mistake, | 81 |

# PROEM.

*Dear Reader:—*

        'Tis the usual thing in prefaces, to shiver
In dread suspense, before the world, the young heart all
    aquiver
With dire fears of this or that, of what the world will
    mutter,
Of what the wisest men will say, or what the critics utter—
It is the usual thing, I say, to kneel, in mortal terror,
And supplicate the reading minds to pardon every error.
Excuse me, reader mine, if I prefer to upright stand,
Or fail to bend the suppliant's knee to any in the land.
If I present these waifs of mine, without a shake or shud-
    der,
And launch my shallop on the deep, without an oar or
    rudder.
I've known full many writers who have sent their crafts
    adrifting
Adown the "rapid river," while their eyes are humbly
    lifting
Unto grim Talus, striding round that dreaded isle of story
Where dwells the fearful Minotaur—the critics grim and
    hoary,

But did their pleadings ever make the heavy club fall
    lighter,
Or soothe his anger e'er a jot, or make their records whiter?
No! no! if Fame is to be ours, it comes all uninvited
And all our coaxing is in vain—for often, when most
    slighted,
We suddenly awake to find the dame has made us noted
Though we have never suppliant been, nor made our-
    selves devoted.
And so I cut adrift my craft, and send it o'er the main,
Contented, if, in time, it should the hoped for landing gain.
Good by, my little shallop, you must your own battle wage.
Farewell, my reader, I am yours,

                Most truly,

                    HANNAH GAGE.

# THE LAND BY THE SUNSET SEA.

IN the country far to westward, in the land of golden fame,
Where the warm hearts melt the ice and the snows are but a name,
There arose a wondrous power, and it lighted all the world,
Till the banners of the Union, in its honor, were unfurled.
From the East, and North, and Southward poured the eager, young and old,
To bow down before this power—for this monarch's name was *Gold*.
Hand in hand, the man of labor and the man to manor born,
Men whose suns were almost setting, youth in freshest hope of morn,
Husbands, fathers, brothers, lovers, sought that far-off "sunset land,"
Where the whispering Pacific kissed the burning golden sands.
Went, with hearts elate with promise, brains with visions great aflame,
Sure of gaining untold riches in this golden land of fame.
Farewell kisses on the faces that to part with left a pain
In the heart, and moistened lashes; but the fever in the veins

Dried the tears, and burned the brighter for the dear ones left behind,
While, through bearded lips there fluttered half-formed prayers upon the wind.
But they found that infant country overgrown with forests bold;
Found that wealth meant honest labor, for the eager young and old.
Found no sceptred monarch ruling all the country miles around;
Found that but to kneel before him, they must dig beneath the ground.
But, unconquered and undaunted, fell they to with lusty will—
Stroke of ax and sound of sawing in the forest grand–until
All those giants who for ages had withstood the tempests blast,
With a crash of parting branches, at their feet lay prone at last.
Then they built their rough log cabins from the fallen giants' limbs.
Faces tanned and weather-beaten, seen 'neath broad *sombrero* brims,
"Hearts of oak and and nerves of sinew," purpose firm and ready hand
Ever to a brother offered in this golden "sunset land."
But, when work of day was ended, and around their rude hearth fires,

Groups of tired men were clustered — husbands, brothers,
    lovers, sires —
Then, amid a sacred silence, men who had not wept for
    years,
Pulled their hats low down to cover manly eyes bedimmed
    with tears;
And the distant dear ones, waiting, watching, hoping,
    praying there,
Might have felt, across the ocean, a low-spoken, fervent
    prayer;
Might have felt that, though between them rolled an
    ocean wild and wide,
Love could span the weary distance, love could laugh at
    wind and tide.
Some with life and hope refulgent, sought this land of
    promise fair,
But, away from home and kindred, to lay down their burden
    there.
With no soothing hand of woman on the aching forehead
    lain,
When the heart was tired and homesick and the head
    was hot with pain.
Only bearded faces gathered round their weary, dying
    mate
Till he passed away, in silence, through an unseen "Golden
    Gate."
Rough the times and rough the justice, meted out to er-
    ring man;

Rough the life and rough the country; rough the race that
    many ran;
Rough the ways and rough the people; rough, alas! the
    morals, too;
Rough the voices, rough the language of this pioneering
    crew—
Yet this land of golden promise grew and prospered, till,
    where stood
Huts and cabins in the clearings made through forest land
    and wood
Cities rose, in size and power, soon to take their stand beside
Elder sisters o'er the ocean, over on the eastern side.
Now, throughout our glorious nation she can claim an
    honored place;
Sister States, throughout the Union, know and recognize
    her face.
She can call each elder "sister," claim a younger kindred's
    stand,
In the Union, proud and happy, can this glorious "sunset
    land."
We, her sons, are proud to call her "Mother"—proud to
    muster here,
On her wedding day. Oh, Mother! turn to us thy listen-
    ing ear;
Hear the praises that thy children o'er thy head will grate-
    ful sing.
Turn thy loving eyes upon us, while thy wedding bells
    shall ring.

Though the ocean wild shall part us, though the wide world
    lay between.
Still our hearts will mock at distance; still we'll keep thy
    memory green.
Still thy love will be our mentor, though the ceaseless ages
    roll,
Mother, sacred, sacred Mother! Alma mater of our soul!

## RETROSPECTION.

LOOKING back o'er the sinuous ways;
　Looking back at the yesterdays,
What does it show us?　Fair or sad?
Does it bring the tears, or the heart-leaps glad?
Looking back at the days agone—
Much to gladden—ah! much to mourn!
Part the curtains of Mem'ry's Hall,
Down the dim vista voices call.
Voices of dear ones, "gone before"—
Sweeter than aught in present lore.
Curtained alcoves, on either side,
The dim, old Hall in parts divide.
Curtains of every kind and hue
Conceal their mem'rys, old and new.
Here it is crimson—and behind,
Warm hearts; true loves; kind words enshrined
Golden and blue—pause ye awhile—
Soft! 'Tis only an infant's smile.
Here are a group of childhood's hours;
And here a bunch of faded flowers;
A sister's love; a mother's face;
A smile; a look; a last embrace;

## RETROSPECTION.

A broken fan; a lock of hair;
A kiss; a promise treasured there.
A sable pall falls gloomy, now
It hides, alas! a broken vow.
And here are smiles; and here are tears;
The fancied cares of childhood's years;
Those snowy folds conceal from view
Two sweet, sad eyes, of Heaven's blue.
A cheery laugh, that broke the spell—
But that was years ago—ah! well!—
And, here and there, a friendly nod;
A face now resting 'neath the sod;
And smiles; and tears; and words of cheer;
And long lost faces, treasured dear,
Peep out, and mystic voices call
Adown dear mem'ry's hallowed Hall.
And last, this alcove, draped in blue,
Its color signifying *true*—
Conceals a Friendship, firm and tried,
Prized higher than all else beside—
'Twas made in Sunshine, tried in storm—
The heart that holds it is large and warm.
When Fortune's bubble, great and fair,
Burst, and left naught but vaporous air;
And so-called "friends" had fled, aghast
At the woeful wreck of Failure's blast,
'Twas *then* the first, firm plank was laid,
Of this blue alcove—sacred made

To Friendship—and though blasts may rock
This frame—it can sustain the shock.
It fears no fate, while firm and true,
Stands Friendship, in this alcove blue.
"Only a *friend!*" Aye, *only*—true!
But enough to pass one safely through—
And blest, indeed, if in Mem'ry's store
You've *only a friend*, and nothing more.

## A THOUGHT.

ALL day long in my mind has lingered
    A sweet, sad thought that I could not name
All day long has the spirits fingered
A golden harp as they went and came
Went and came, and the harp strings throbbing,
Low and sad as an angel sobbing,
Told the thought that I could not name—
Softly sung what I could not name.

Vainly reaching, I tried to clasp it
Clasp the harp with its golden strings,
Tried in my rude, world hands to grasp it,
That I might tell of the beautiful things
My heart could sing, but my lips not utter,
Timed to the murmur of rippling water,
But they denied me those golden strings,
Coldy refused me those golden strings.

That is why, though my heart is singing,
I cannot tell what I think or feel,
That is why with the music ringing
Through my brain, I but dumbly kneel,
Kneel to the beautiful thought held captive,
'Tween the walls of this brain a captive
Striving to tell what I think or feel,
Vainly striving to tell what I feel.

## TWO VIEWS OF LIFE.

*The Cynic's.*

TOILING along o'er the dusty road,
Toiling along till we're worn, and old
Always the weight of a heavy load,
Necessity urging us on like a goad.

Toiling and striving, always the same,
Whether for bread, for gold or for fame,
Friendship's a mockery, love but a name,
Burning out life with its lurid flame.

Some are born fortunate—plainly not I,
Hopes, aspirations, end in a sigh.
No art or luring can coax Fortune nigh;
Why should I longer live?  Far better die.

Life's not worth living—better 'twould be
That I should end it; plunge in the sea!
Anywhere! so from this world to be free.
Free to lie down in Eternity.

*The Worker's.*

Is the road dusty? do we grow old?
Are we all grovelling for silver and gold?
Are none of us kindly, all of us cold?
Is everyone's heart to be bartered and sold?

Is love a mockery? have we no friend?
Must we strive singly on to the end?
Is no one trying his wrong ways to mend?
No one contented? hearts made but to rend?

Is life a failure for those who try?
Does no one hear the heart's anguished cry?
Is death a Lethe? is there no tie
Binding to earth, though 'tis clasped with a sigh?

Is death the end? Who of us knows!
Better bear bravely this life and its woes;
Judging not, taking the world as it goes;
Willing, with patience, to wait for the close.

## THE HAPPY MEDIUM.

I LOVED, and the world was all peopled with angels,
No face that I met looked unkind unto me.
The skies were all bright, and the sunlight all golden,
The gull's call was music, away out at sea.
The robins that sang in the tree-tops were joyous;
The lamb's bleat, the dog's bark, each, each was in tune,
I extended my foes all a hand of good feeling.
Oh, the darkest of night seemed the highest of noon.

I hated—the world was a world full of demons.
No face there but harbored a treacherous lie.
The skies were as midnight—the sun's face was hidden,
I shrank from the scream of the seagulls near by.
The voice of the robin was harsh and discordant,
The lamb's bleat was savage—the dog's bark a howl.
I forgave not a foe, and with bent head and angry
I passed all my friends, with a dark sullen scowl.

But, a change came, a subtile, refining, deep influence
Crept into my life, and I scarcely knew how.
It stayed my impatience, and softened my anger—
Till I cannot, and will not dispense with it now.
A cool hand was laid on my hot, aching forehead,
It smoothed out the wrinkles, and bade me attend.
I caught it, and kissed it, and gratefully murmured
That word, of all words the most beautiful—"*Friend.*"

## A KISS.

A HEART looked out from its prison bars,
And gazed, enrapt, on its chosen mate—
But no words uttered the love it bore,
And it sighed in pain to its unkind fate:
"Oh fate, most cruel! Why give me love
And deny me the power to make it known?
Oh, but to kneel at my idol's feet,
And pour out the story to her alone!"

A heart looked back in the tender eyes;
And blushed, not knowing the reason why,
But guessing half—yet were words too bold
To tell that her spirit had heard the cry.
Two hearts estranged for a missing link,
A magic clasp to the golden chain—
Just wanting this must the secret still
In the two hearts' casket, held fast, remain?

Two hands have met in a silent clasp,
And eyes met eyes in a long, long look—
It is almost told, but there's something yet,
For the bridge is lacking to span the brook.
Eyes draw nearer, heart beats 'gainst heart,
Unheeded, unneeded the harsh words cold—
From heart to heart has its secret passed,
In the first long *kiss* it was fully told.

## A PICTURE.

'TIS a face of wonderful beauty,
    That looks from its walnut frame,
The eyes are deeply, tenderly dark—
    Their beauty I could not name.

The hair is short, but of finest silk.
    And brown as a chestnut burr;
And its curls in rings around the head,
    Far softer than softest fur.

The lips, just parted, reveal behind
    Two rows of *whitest* teeth;
Oh! who can look in that pictured face,
    And doubt of the heart beneath?

Aye! the face of a trusted, long-tried friend!
    A friend, *not* "a friend for a day,"
Is the pictured face before me—
    The face of our old dog, Tray.

## THE KISS.

HE kissed me—yes; you need not smile,
He kissed me, and I felt, the while,
A thrill of joy, exquisite bliss,
Creeping o'er me, as I met his kiss.

He kissed me, and 'twas all I knew,
His eyes; twin stars of truest blue,
That shone alone, I know, for me,
Met mine in loving loyalty.

He kissed me—thrilling thro' me came
A feeling that I could not name.
That dear, dear face ! No other could
Throughout the world, be half so good.

His kisses and his words are more
To me, than all the world before,
Oh, dearer far than aught or other,
My treasure-trove—my baby brother!

## ONLY A BROKEN ROSEBUD.

Only a broken rosebud,
    Carelessly thrown aside;
  That had lost its way
  From the small bouquet,
    That hung by my lady's side.

Only a broken rosebud,
    Dying neglected there—
  In the throes of death,
  The fragrant breath
    Perfuming the heated air.

Only a broken rosebud
    Snatched from the cruel tread,
  And the careless beat
  Of the dancer's feet,
    As they swept above its head.

Only a broken rosebud,
    Clasped to a broken heart,
  Passionate kisses,
  Wild tears and wishes—
    "Forever and aye apart!"

Only a broken rosebud
    Carefully laid away,
  In its faded shroud,
  From the heat and crowd,
    Like a youthful hope grown gray.

Only a broken rosebud
    Withered before its time,
  Faded and gray,
  In its youthful day,
    Yellowed and dead in its prime.

Only a broken rosebud,
    Lost from the rest, unwept,
  But to me 'tis frought
  With a hallowed thought,
    And with sacred sadness kept.

## SKATING.

NIGHT on the frozen water, and from a haven close
　　Between two jutting boulders, the curling smoke
　　　　arose.
Fair Luna's car a casket seemed, filled to excess with stars,
And, glimmering 'tween the golden sparks, the silvery
　　　　moon beam bars.
The skaters, muffled to the eyes, went wheeling graceful
　　　　o'er
The glassy surface, here and there, along the icy floor,
And, over all, Queen Luna's Car so nobly rode the blue—
While merry laughter, jest, and song rung loud the clear
　　　　air through.
Ah, skating is delightful sport, the liveliest and the best.
In sweet concord the heavens above—the waters 'neath at
　　　　rest.
Who would not be a skater, in a party made of two?
Spurning the ice-bound river—"Some other one" and you.
If you have never tried it, take my advice, and go,
When in the haven ice has formed, you'll not regret, I know.
Go! Go! once there, and I'll engage no art or luring then
Can coax you from that "others" side, back 'mongst your
　　　　fellow men.

## WRITTEN ON THE FLY-LEAF OF MY DIARY.

WITHIN this book, my curious friend,
    Restrain your eyes from peeping.
There's nothing here I'd care to lose,
And nothing worth your keeping.
Of sage, old Wisdom's wondrous store,
I've borrowed scanty measure,
'Tis all my own—this motley lore,
Culled from my brain, at leisure.
And what is here concerns but me—
'Tis no one else's matter,
If "Cousin Jane" drops in to tea,
Or Bridget breaks a platter.
'Tis *mine*, and mine alone, to con
These pages, closely written,
And he who dares to look upon
Them, may be sadly bitten.
If eyes *will* scan forbidden ground,
And peep between these pages,
I call upon the country round,
And all the wise, old sages—
To bear me out—that if they find
Opinions plainly stated,

And close the book with bitter mind,
And feelings not elated—
'Tis not *my* fault—I warned them off,
They heeded not my warning,
They took no notice, but to scoff
And jeer with wilful scorning.
So bid the tempest go his way,
My friend, you'll not regret it—
But, there! I've done, I've said my say
Be sure you don't forget it.

## UNSPOKEN THOUGHTS.

I AM sitting alone with my musings to-night,
  In the room where I've done all my thinking—
With only the gleam of subdued firelight—
And the past with the present time linking.

Here are wont to assemble, the ghosts of the past—
Here I'm wont to live over once more
The scenes and the pleasures, too sweet far to last,
And again meet the lost friends of yore.

But to-night I'm not dreaming of days that are dead
But of thoughts that my wild heart is burning
To tell—but alas! they will never be said—
Every effort they long have been spurning.

Oh! to call up the spirits and bid them attend—
To bid them enchant my dull pencil—
A magical power its movements to lend,
That the beautiful thoughts I may stencil.

Alas! there are songs that will never be sung,
Songs too sweet for the cruel world's listening—
There are silvery bells that will never be rung—
Tho' we see in the distance their glistening.

Be content then, oh heart, be content just to *think*
Of what others so vainly have sought—
Be content if the Muses allow you to drink
From the crystaline " Fountain of Thought."

## "HALF - MAST."

A SHIP swung proud in the lower bay,
   Awaiting her master to sail away;
While he on the shore, said a parting word
To his blue-eyed love—but the wavelets heard
The long, long kiss on her fond lips pressed,
While the ship lay tossing in wild unrest.
And only the wind, as it whispered low,
And the waves' retreat, with its muffled beat,
Could tell of the brave young captain's vow.

The ship sailed out from the harbor white,
With its spread of sail, in a glow of light;
And the blue eyes watched from the wave-beat shore,
As the good ship on to her journey bore.
And the captain back, 'neath his shading hand,
Gazed to the fast receding land.
Then turned, when the shore grew a tiny speck,
To his duties great, and the captain's mate
Smiled to himself, as he paced the deck.

Time rolled on and the day had come
When the maiden would welcome her sailor home.
Into the harbor the good ship sailed.
Home, at last! But the bright cheek paled—

For the mate was pacing the deck alone,
And when to its bed was the anchor thrown,
The mate alone from the vessel stepped,
And the waves were sobbing, in anguish throbbing,
While the winds a mournful monody wept.

The flag, aloft, at half mast hung.
Through the air, despairing, a wild cry rung.
A crowd of people, a wan face white,
Two blue eyes veiled from the cold world's sight.
Kind arms bore her back home again,
Kind hearts softened the cruel pain,
Kind words soothingly bade her brave
The cruel dart in her bleeding heart,
The thought of the far-off ocean grave.

She did not die—how few e'er do?
But every day by the water blue,
She watched for the ship and its captain brave,
And wept o'er the lonely ocean grave.
One day they found her, with whitened locks,
Washed by the water among the rocks,
And they knew the captain's love, at last,
Had crossed the strand to the far-off land,
And entered port, with her flag half-mast.

## A FACE.

THERE's a face that comes when cares oppress,
   And my life is weary and sad;
It comes with its quiet sympathy,
   And makes my whole heart glad.

It is not a comely face, but more
   Is seen in the truthful eyes;
They seem to read my heavy heart,
   And, somehow, my spirits rise.

The world may call it plain, but I,
   Who have learned its truth to read,
Can see in the thoughtful, earnest face
   The friend that is a friend in *deed*.

## KISSES.

I ASKED a child at her busy play
    " Why is your mama's kiss sweet, my child?"
Turning an instant her sport away,
    "'Cause mama loves me," the child replied.

I asked a mother with whitening hair,
    Mending the little garments torn,
"Why is your child's kiss sweet?" the fair
    Face lightened, "She's all my own."

"Can you tell me why a kiss is sweet?"
    I asked of a maiden — "tell me, pray?"
She blushed, refusing my eyes to meet,
    With never a word she turned away.

What is it, but a meeting of lips?
    Wherein lies the ineffable bliss,
Like to the nectar the Love-god sips—
    All in an instant, born in a kiss.

## LIFE.

LIFE is not what many dub it—
   All a fleeting show at best.
Fate is not a hardened cynic,
Our best efforts to arrest.

Why should we, but toiling mortals—
Striving for the topmost round—
Think to reach it, think to gain it,
Only one step from the ground.

Ah, ye haughty! ah, ye proud hearts!
Ye must learn the lesson all—
Up to Fame, or up to Glory,
Hand o'er hand we all must crawl.

Crawl, aye, *crawl*, ye sons of freedom,
Naught we gain without some tears,
Many tumbles, many bruises,
Many backward steps, and fears.

Should you fail in climbing upward,
Try again,—'tis not too late—
Do not grapple with the goddess—
No one ever conquered Fate.

If it is to be, why let it—
Bear the ill winds with the good;
Do not shun life's jagged corner—
You could round them if you would.

Come what will, let's meet it bravely
With our hearts on triumph set,
And we'll soon be thinking: "Truly,
Life is *not* a failure yet."

## A FRIEND IN NEED.

A THIRSTY flower, parched and dry
    Lay dying in the grass—
In vain for water did it sigh,
    Relief came not. "Alas!
And must I thus neglected die?"
    The flower murmuring said,
"And must I thirsting, parching lie,
    Unwept, uncared for—dead?"
"Sweet flower," spoke a liquid voice,
    "Thou shalt not perish so.
Lift up thy head—revive! rejoice!
    Thy bud shall live to blow.
Quaff thou this drop of dew, new born,
    And thou shall live to see
The sun rise high on many a morn.
    Up! live! move and be free!"
The soft voice ceased, the flower—face
    Up-turned in wonder sweet
A dew-drop, with its modest grace,
    Stooped down its lips to meet.
It quaffed, and soon in beauteous bloom
    Its fragrance, pure and rare,
Sweet thanks for its escape from doom,
    Up floated on the air.

## THE EAGLE.—*A Sonnet.*

ATOP the lofty mountain grimly stands,
    Silent above his winged, feathered flock,
Immovable as is the the massive rock,
The king of all the smaller feathered bands,
With piercing eye he looks o'er all the lands,
Then down, where many jagged boulders block
The way, and straggling creepers interlock,
Then tighter grasps the rock, with mighty hands
And flapping wide his wings against his side,
He plumes his feathers, and with hooked beak
He combs his plumage to a glittering black,
With one keen glance around the country wide,
Down casts his body from the lofty peak
In circling curves, pursues his chosen track.

## JAMES A. GARFIELD.

### 1880.

BENEATH the Nation's banner, wide unfurled
    To do him honor, stands the man we choose
To quell all wrong, to uphold right—our foes
To conquer—Lo ! he stands before the world
Our chosen ruler—At his feet, down hurled,
The vulture Fraud—aye ! every freeman knows
His upright bearing—that his record shows.
When smoke of battle from our homes up-curled,
His arm was foremost in our Union's cause.
And, now, when war's wild trumpet blast is still,
And Justice rules the realm, she hard has earned—
O'er our free Nation, ruler of her laws,
We raise this man. Ye people do his will !
On every heart may Garfield's name be burned.

## NAN.

A BLAZE of gaslight, a faint perfume, a sea of heads and a fan,
A hum of voices, a trembling tune—this is all, since the ball began,
All I have known, or have heeded, of the glitter, the fuss and the crush,
For, 'midst it all, I am conscious still, of a half-embarassed hush,
While Nan is bending her lovely head, and pulling the petals apart,
Of a milk-white rose. Do those fingers know they are pulling to pieces a heart?
Oh, for the days, when, a cavalier brave, I could sing of chivilric deeds?
Oh, to be knight of her chosen love, that her errant heart must needs
Be warmed to life by this love of mine, that is burning my heart away!
Oh, cruel Nan, to refuse the balm, that could all this pain allay!
Oh, cruel Nan, to demurly stand, with your beautiful eyes down-cast,

And torture that rose that has done no harm, while my
    breath comes comes thick and fast.
Oh, for the courage to ask for what I would barter my
    my life to win!
One word, a whisper—it would be done—but I know not
    how to begin.
And so I bend to the lovely head, and whisper—low, 'tis
    true—
But, 'tis only a common-place, after all,—"May I have
    this dance with you?"

## WINDING UP TIME.

A WEE, brown maid on a door-step sat,
   Her small face hid 'neath a wide-brimmed hat ;
A broken clock on her baby knee,
She wound with an ancient, rusty key.
" What are you doing, my pretty one?
Playing with Time?" I asked in fun.
Large and wise were the soft, dark eyes,
Lifted to mine in a grave surprise.
" I'se windin' him up, to make him go,
For he's so drefful pokey and slow."
Winding up Time? Ah, baby mine !
How crawl these lengthened moments of thine ;
How sadly slow goes the staid old man ;
But he has not changed since the world began.
*He* does not change, but, in after years,
When he mingles our cup of joy with tears ;
When the day is too short for its crowd of cares,
And night surprises us, unawares,
We will not wish to hurry his feet,
But find his going all too fleet.

Ah, baby mine! Some future day,
You will throw that rusted key away,
And to Phœbus's car will madly cling,
As it whirs along, like a winged thing,
And wonder, how, years and years ago,
You could ever have thought that Time was slow.

## BIRDIE.

BIRDIE, oh Birdie! Why, what are you saying,
  Swinging so fast on that slender, young bough?
Do you not fear that a price you'll be paying,
For telling bad boys where your home-nest is now?
Do you find, Birdie, that this earth is sweet enough?
Have you ne'er fear that some trouble will come?
Come in a way that is startling, and oh, so rough!
Robbing you, Birdie, of children and home?
What are you thinking of, with your small, saucy head
Tilted up sidewise, with wide-open eye?
Is it of baby birds safe in their downy bed?
Are you first listening for their shrill cry?
Birdie, oh Birdie! my heart is o'erflowing
With mirth— you're so funny, so solemn and small,
Such a wee mother, important and glowing,
Sharp little ears for her baby-birds' call.

## KRIS KRINGLE.

NIGHT came down o'er an English town,
    Half hid 'tween mountains of glistening white—
And the villagers drew into a knot, for they knew
    Kris Kringle would pay them a visit that night.

As the sun went down over all the town,
    Rung the curfew bell, and the lights went out—
While the children sped to their humble bed,
    With a sidewise look and a glance about,

Half hoping they might catch a fleeting sight
    Of the broad, red face, with its genial smile—
And the twinkling eye, with its wink so sly—
    And the sleigh and tiny reindeer, the while,

The village slept, and the moon had crept
    Up to the zenith, and, all around,
Shed is its rays in a dreamy haze,
    On the snow-clad hill, and the whitened ground.

As the clock struck twelve, a minature elve
  Sprang from the earth, and resounded long
A winding note from a bugle throat,
  And from every spot sprung a glittering throng

Of fairies light, in their robes of white,
  Bearing their queen on a coach of ice,
Dancing each side of the coach with pride—
  That was drawn by twelve silky and snow-white mice.

Merrily danced the elves, and pranced
  Down through the center, then back again.
Glittering white in the pale moonlight—
  So merrily danced the fairy train.

These were the sprites of the Christmas rites,
  That the legend tells us are always known,
At the mystic hour when the old church tower
  Re-echoes the midnight bell's deep tone.

At the height of fun, when the sprites begun
  To lead their queen to a dancer's place,
On the air afloat, came a distant note,
  A tinkle of bells, and each fairy's face

Wore a listening look, then their leader shook
  Her scepter, and pointed, in quick command,
To the topmost peak of the mountain bleak,
  Where sky stooped down to salute the land.

For there appeared, and each moment neared
   The group, a sleigh and twelve tiny reindeer.
Or, to be brief, 'twas the Christmas chief—
   Old jolly Kris Kringle, with merry cheer.

The elf-queen sprung to her chariot, swung
   The mice around, and her signal gave—
The clarion rung from the bugle tongue :
   "Up elves ! and away to your sovereign brave.

A moment more, and Kris Kringle bore
   Swift down from the mountain, with steaming deer.
And they pranced along to the merry throng,
   Who met the king with a ringing cheer.

The queen's white mice, in a merry trice,
   Had drawn her beside the old king's sleigh,
And the sprightly elves had ensconced themslves
   On deer and chariot, and up, away !

Over the snow-bound earth they go.
   Down the chimnies, and everywhere—
Filling a stocking, without unlocking
   A door, go Kris and his lady fair.

At last the sleigh being empty, they
   Recalled their elves, who had helped unload,
And turning the mice and deer, in a trice,
   Were speeding backward along the road.

And, as they went, the old king bent
  A backward look on the sleeping town,
And waved his hand o'er the white-robed land,
  "Good will to all! And peace come down!"

And, in a trice, the deer and mice,
  The king and queen, and their merry band,
Had vanished quite, and the frosty night
  Quietly settled o'er all the land.

## CHRISTMAS EVE.

ALL nature slept beneath a spread
   Of whitest, softest snow, o'er head
The blue expanse was studded bright
With stars—The soft-eyed Queen of Night
Rode silent in her silver car,
As if, perchance, a voice would jar
The slumbering earth. The trees weighed down
With limbs of snow, and whitened crown,
Stood motionless, like sentinels,
On Christmas eve—The town clock tells
Eleven—the moon-lit, frosty air
Was still as death, dull toil and care
Were sleeping, and the shadows lay
Athwart the ground in grim array,
As slowly round the dial crept
The minute hand, and passed, unwept,
The quarter hour, and then the half—
Three-quarters—and as yet, the chaff
Of thistle down would not be stirred
By any breath could yet be heard

Ten minutes, five, four, three, two, one.
The Christmas morning is near begun.
All sudden on the silence rung
A joyous peal, caught up, and flung
Upon the air by many a bell
Who would the gladsome birthday tell.
Flung high and far in ringing peals,
As if each bell the glory feels.
Echoed by mountain, hill and glen,
"Peace be on earth, good will toward men!"

## CHRISTMAS.

A TINKLING of bells on the frosty air ;
A whir of runners ; a gladsome laugh ;
Two wee blackbirds in the snow out there ;
A burst of music, and merry chaff.

I know that Christmas is coming fast ;
I hear the sleigh on the roof above ;
I hear, in the wind, his trumpet blast ;
And I know he is off on his path of love.

I know the signs that his heralds bring ;
I feel the touch of his frosty breath ;
I hear his laugh in the church bell's ring ;
His sigh in the frost-nipt flowers' death.

I catch the gleam of his twinkling eye,
In the dancing flames of the hearthfire's glow ;
And his face, in the snowy sky,
And his ermine robe, in the mantling snow.

So pile the logs, let the flame leap higher,
That, when he comes from the outside cold,
He may warm himself by the blazing fire,
For dear Kris Kringle is growing old.

There are lines of care on his ruddy face,
There are deep "crow's-feet" by his laughing eyes.
Two thousand years has he led our race,
We will meet *him* now with a great surprise.

And, when he has warmed his frozen toes,
Into his mittens he'll quickly pop—
And, as up the chimney he deftly goes,
Will call "Good night!" from the chimney-top.

## NEW YEAR'S EVE.

ANOTHER year will be closed to-night,
    Another link to the chain ;
A day gone by in every life—
    A sheaf of the garnered grain.
Another thread in the warp and woof,
    That is wrapping our lives around—
Another strand to the checkered ball
    That from every life is wound—
A finished page in the "Book of Life,"
    Another leaf turned down.
A dress of rags or a purple robe,
    A bed of straw, or a crown.
It is all the same to the bent old man
    Who has kept the record true,
Of the past twelve months of every life,
    By moments the record grew.
And now we stand by his dying couch,
    And watch the flickering light,
As it comes and goes in a fitful way,
    Through the weary hours of night.

It is almost twelve, and the old man's breath
    Is growing fainter, and chill,
The damp has gathered in beaded drops,
    The breathing is almost still.
Silent we wait while the minutes speed,
    And midnight is drawing nigh.
Over his features a shadow steals,
    And he breathes a labored sigh.
Almost twelve—through the winter's night
    A sound of music comes—
A silvery peal of fife and horn,
    And the rattling roll of drums.
A childish face, and a snow white robe,
    In the room—and the bell outpealed
Twelve—while the sweet new-comer came,
    And down by the bedside kneeled.
The dim eyes opened a moment, then,
    And the feeble hand outheld
The "Book of Records" and the hour-glass,
    A look that would volumes tell.
"I trust to you the coming year"—
    That look of meaning said—
And sinking back, with a tired sigh,
    The dear Old Year was dead.

## MY CALLER.

ONLY *one* caller this New Year;
    For I live in a quiet street;
  And am all unknown
  To the busy throng,
That make up the world's elite.

Only *one* caller this New Year,
But *my* caller stayed all day—
  And the sand slipped through
  The hour-glass, too,
In a *very* old fashioned way.

Before the grate, red blazing,
It may be silence fell—
  But, if it was so,
  Or whether, or no,
Do you think I'm going to tell.

I can see from my cottage window
A mansion on Grandee street;
  And can hear the rush,
  The hurry and crush,
And the tramp of Fashion's feet.

But I do not envy the many
That are calling there to-day,
   I am well content
   That the gods have sent
*One* caller along this way.

Only *one* called this New Year—
But my *one* sufficed for all
   The hundred and more
   That passed my door
On their way to Fashion's hall.

Let them count their cards and conquests,
I am content with mine—
   Let them smile and boast
   And drink the toast
In the deep of the sparkling wine.

My single caller is all enough,
*They* may think I covet the rest
   The many calls,
   The parties and balls,
But my caller and I know best.

## NEW YEAR'S CALLERS.

CALLERS and callers, and wine and cake,
    And every degree of nervous hand shake.
Some will bow with a languid air,
A critical note of my dress and hair.
Others bend o'er my white-gloved hand
And murmur, faintly, a sentence bland.
My right arm aches with the tedious strain
And my head is splitting in two with the pain.
And it's only five o'clock—just think !
Six more hours of healths to drink,
Hundreds more to be met, and hear
The same old commonplace in my ear.
The same " so happy" and " many returns "—
A smile, a bow, the tormentor turns
To give his place to another—ah me,
And is this the " world " I came to see?
Is *this* the brilliant, the "fashion world?"
Its only aim to be lightly whirled
Thro' a gaslit room, or to grinning stand,
And bow and caper and offer your hand

## NEW YEAR'S CALLERS.

To hundreds whose faces you cannot recall,
And is this the brilliant fashion and all?
Ah me to stand, on New Year's day,
In the old, bright parlor, so far away—
And wait, betwixt dinner and supper, to hear
A ringing voice, with its hearty cheer.
I did not covet the many calls,
Or the numerous parties and balls
When I stood in the doorway, a year ago,
And received my caller from out of the snow.
I did not envy the parties a bit,
When the glow of the wood fire lit
The chestnut curls and the laughing face,
That the head of the proudest king would grace.
And I miss that face from the smirking throng
That have nodded and bustled the whole day long.
I like the money and all it brings,
But the dressing, fussing, and calling rings
With a spurious sound; and instead of men,
With hearts and souls, I feel, time and again,
As if we were dolls, made after the same,
Identical patterns, save just in name.
I thought how grand it would be to shine
In a circle of "upper ten," and dine
With the "best select," when I was told
I was left sole heiress to heaps of gold.

## NEW YEAR'S CALLERS.

Ah me! ah me! it is wisely said
That uneasy must lie the crowned head.
I would give it all—but who can be
That tall young fellow approaching me?
So much unlike the "puppet men,"
I have met with a greeting, time and again.
It is—no!—yes!—am I awake.
Those soft, dark eyes and the warm hand shake,
And the chestnut curls—my best of friends,
For all my trials this makes amends.
My caller of just a year ago—
Who came to me through the driving snow.
Of course he is only a *friend*, but then
He makes me feel myself again.

## ONLY FRIENDS.

A MANLY fellow, straight and tall—
A wee, brown maiden, dainty, small;
Two eyes of gray, two eyes of brown—
Gray eyes in dark—brown eyes look down;
A small plump hand, held frankly out;
A mouth, that half suggests a pout,
Has framed the simple words, "Good-bye;"
The manly lips likewise reply;
She laughs—he smiles—and then hands meet—
A nod—"Good-bye"—he's down the street.
He meets a friend—"I say, old boy,
How's pretty Minnie—dainty, coy?
Come don't deny, dear fellow; say!
*I* saw your parting—plain as day."
"By Jove! my boy, you're going mad,
Your ignorance is really sad.
Miss Minnie? Why I've not in town
So old a friend as Minnie Brown!
That's rich, by Jove! too rich, by half!
I'll tell't to Min; 'twill make her laugh."

A friend of Minnie also saw
The friendly parting at the door ;
"Come! Minnie, tell me when 'twill be.
Now don't look stupid ; folks can see
That you're engaged to Edward Ames.
Now, don't be cross and call bad names,
I saw your parting at the door ;
'Twas proof enough—I want no more.
But Minnie raised her honest eyes,
And said in genuine surprise :
"We're only friends, Ned Ames and I ;
I've known him since I was *so* high.
The idea never crossed my mind
That aught but friendship folks could find
In all I've said to him, or he
Has said in fun or truth to me.
I'll tell him when he comes to-day—
The dear old fellow—what folks say—
He'll laugh, I guess, to think, forsooth,
Folks guess so very far from truth.
He came. "O Ned ! the queerest news
I heard to-day from Clara Dawes !"
" Not half so funny, Min, as I
Was told to-day by Franklyn Nye."
" Wait, Ned ; let me tell first," she said.
" Dear me ! You'd never guess it, Ned."

She said—"oh, dear! those stupid boors.
I guess I'll tell mine last—tell yours."
"Well, Min, Frank Nye was trying to chaff
About—by Jove, it made me laugh—
About, you know—say, Min, can't you
Tell me yours first? Now, how'll that do?"
"Oh, never mind—'tis best unsaid.
You wouldn't care to hear it, Ned."
"Oh, yes I would. But I'll tell first
My news. Prepare, Min, for the worst!
Well, here it is: He said—Frank Nye—
That we were 'spoony,' you and I."
"Oh, Ned how strange! Why that's what she—
I mean Miss Clara, told to me."
"No, Min. By Jove! the deuce it is!
So her news was the same as his?
What bosh! Enough of this. I've come
To tell you I shall soon leave home
To stay a year—most likely two.
I say, what makes you look so blue?
Tears, Min? Good gracious! what's up now?
Come tell a fellow what's the row?"
"I—I—'tis nothing—truly—Ned—
But—don't go—stay at home instead."
Two flushed, red cheeks, two dark-brown eyes—
Two gray eyes opened in surprise—

The gray eyes meet the eyes of brown;
The brown eyes droop their lashes down.
A pause, and then a whisle low,
" By George !—well, Min, I didn't know—"
But *something* cut the sentence short—
Two pouting lips tried to retort,
The manly lips refused the quest—
I'll leave you now to guess the rest.

A manly fellow, straight and tall,
A wee, brown maiden, dainty, small,—
Two eyes of gray—two eyes of brown—
Gray eyes in dark—brown eyes look down.
A small, plump hand held firmly in
A larger palm. " My darling Min !"
Again is breathed a low " good-bye "—
A scarcely audible reply,
" Folks weren't *very* wrong, hey, Min?
I guess 'twas *we* were ' taken in,'
But if they hadn't guessed the truth,
We'd never known ourselves, forsooth."

## WAITING FOR SANTA CLAUS.

BEYOND the curtain's crimson light,
Is still and fair, the winter night;
Wrapt in her ermine robe she lies,
Asleep beneath the snowy skies,
Above peep down the twinkling stars,
Between the slanting moon-beam bars,
    One Christmas Eve.

A bright fire in the open grate;
The stockings all expectant wait;
The household pets sleep on the rug,
Canine and feline, social, snug;
A spicy smell of evergreen,
A gentle hush o'er every thing,
    That Christmas Eve.

Upstairs, within her little bed,
A child raised up her golden head,
And slyly ope'd her saucy eyes,
And glanced around, and nodded wise;

Then softly slipped upon the floor,
And slyly ope'd her chamber door,
    That Christmas Eve.

Then, round about her childish form,
She wrapt a blanket, thick and warm,
And, noiseless, down the stair-case crept,
To where her hairy playmates slept.
Behind her softly closed the door,
And down she sank upon the floor,
    That Christmas Eve.

The big Newfoundland raised his eyes,
And far too sleepy for surprise,
Gave with his tail a tap or two ;
The cat looked mildly "How d' do?"
Then quietly to dozing fell,
Before the fire's drowzy spell,
    That Christmas Eve.

Down snuggled close the child, beside
The big Newfoundland's shaggy hide,
"I'ze tum to watch for Santa Claus,"
She whispered in his ear, "because

I wote a letter all myself,
And sent it," said the little elf,
   That Christmas Eve.

"Of tourse I touldn't use a pen,
So mama held my hand, and zen
I told him 'zactly what to bring—
And when I hear his sleighbells ring
I'ze doin' to hide away, for fear
He wouldn't tum if I was here,
   On Twismas Eve.

But—but—oh dear! I wish he'd tum!
I asked for brover Ned a dwum,
And—and——" the golden head lay fair,
Against the faithful dog's rough hair,
The eyelids drooped. On Nature's breast
The little one was hushed to rest,
   That Christmas Eve.

Upon the roof a patter came,
Like swiftly falling drops of rain,
And down the chimney quickly popped,
A stout old man, who briskly hopped

## WAITING FOR SANTA CLAUS.

Upon the fender, gazed around,
Then softly stepped upon the ground,
    That Christmas Eve.

The dog looked up with kindly eyes,
The tabbies gazed in mild surprise,
While down was swung the monstrous pack
The old man carried on his back ;
And, at a signal from his hand,
From out his pockets sprang a band,
    That Christmas Eve,

Of merry, dancing, prancing elves,
Who, in a twink, ensconced themselves
Upon the pack, and quick begun
To fill the stockings, one by one,
Old Santa Claus, in glancing round,
Espied the child upon the ground,
    That Christmas Eve.

"Oh, ho ! what have we here?" said he,
"Been trying to catch a glimpse of me,
And while on guard, fell fast asleep?
My pretty one, your slumber keep,

And Santa Claus, and all his band,
Will follow you to Slumber-land,
    This Christmas Eve."

He softly touched the waxen lids,
"My followers, do as Santa bids!"
And, gathering up his lessened pack,
He quickly strapped it on his back,
And followed by his elfin throng,
Skipped up the chimney, and was gone,
    That Christmas Eve.

And when we found her childish form
Wrapt in the blanket, snug and warm,
Her ripe lips parted in a smile,
Though locked in slumber deep the while,
We knew Kris Kringle and his band
Had followed her to Slumber-land,
    That Christmas Eve.

## NEW YEAR'S EVE.

THERE'S a beautiful spirit hovering
    Just over our earth to-night,
A roseat flush on the fair, round cheek,
And eyes of a mystic light.

There's a bent old man on the threshold
Who turns back his tired eyes,
O'er the checkered path he has lately trod,
Then up to the star-lit sky,

Where the beautiful spirit hovers,
In its hand a fair white scroll,
On which it will, in the coming year,
Our records all enroll.

The bent old man upreaches,
And clasps with his withered hand
The rosy palm downstretched to his,
And gently draws it to land.

And there in the open doorway
They greet and say farewell,
While out from the old church steeple
Peals forth the gladsome bell.

When the twelve sharp strokes have ended
The bent old man is gone,
And the spirit has crossed the threshold
Of another New Year's morn.

## BABY WISDOM.

BABY Nell at the window pane
   Gazed solemnly out at the driving rain.
With grave reflections the blue eyes fraught,
My darling was lost in profoundest thought.
" Sage old Wisdom has passed," I said,
"And touched his wand to that baby head.
The grim old fellow, now and then,
Passes us older women and men,
To trace a look so wondrous wise,
In the fathomless depths of a baby's eyes.
Problems of moment and questions of fate
Are hidden away 'neath that curly pate."
Then I crossed to the little figure there,
And laid a hand on her sunny hair.
" What do you see but cold and wet
To chain your gaze to the window, pet?"
The eyes were misty with unshed tears,
And grave with a wisdom beyond her years,
As gravely she turned 'round her golden head,
"I'ze wonderin' what makes Dod cwy," she said.

## 1979.

ONE hundred years have rolled away from off Time's lengthened scroll,
And boys have grown to gray-haired sires, and tottered to the goal.
One hundred years since '79—a century ago.
'Twas then my great-great-grandma lived—at least ma told me so.
I found a musty album and a lot of yellow scraps—
To-day, up in the garret, amongst some queer, old traps,
A pile of letters, neatly tied, and dated '76.
'Twas then my great-great-grandpa came and Cupid played his tricks.
The journal's dated '79—it was that year, I'm sure,
Some famous general, Grant, I think, returned from his tour.
And great-great-grandma's sister Sue strewed flowers in his way.
The people all turned out—'twas quite a gala day.
And Edison, and all those men, were famous then, 'tis said.

And yet, they failed in many things that we have done instead.
There's Smith has made an air machine that travels fast as steam,
And Brown and Jones together make their butter without cream.
*Our* walking matches, now-a-days, I'm sure cannot be beat;
Contestants go upon their *hands*, they're not confined to *feet*.
Why Billy Jones, upon his hands, but just the other day,
Made splendid time upon the track, against old Daniel's bay.
And "Webster's Unabridged" was then but two feet square, 'tis said.
Why dictionaries, now-a-days, are large as any bed.
They could not else contain the words that have been coined since then.
Why, the two feet square would not half hold the names of famous men.
And here, among the yellow scraps, is one so old and worn,
I scarce can cull its meaning—the printing's almost gone.
The writer is Charles Warren S——, I can't make out the name.

It must be Stoddard—that young man, who gained such
    fame,
A century and more ago—I think in '81.
At the good old age of eighty-five, they say his course
    was run.
My great-great-grandma, in her time, I'm told, was
    quite a belle,
And at the "Authors' Carnival" she cut a dashing swell,
As Lady Leicester Dudlock, tall, stately, calm and proud,
And here, in this old paper, they ring her praises loud.
Why, just above the mantle, an ancient painting hangs,
With puffs of soft, white, fleecy hair,—and not those
    horrid bangs—
They wore in 1879, that made one look so wild—
And that was great-great-grandmama, when grandma
    was a child.
'Tis not much like the brilliant belle, that queened it over
    hearts—
In those old days of Carnivals, and balls, and Cupid's
    darts.
They say she flirted desperately with George Fitznoodle
    Browne,
And trod on hearts most ruthlessly, and trampled feelings
    down.
And yet, she must have had a heart, for, in that quaint,
    old chest,

I found, wrapt up in lavender, deep in its velvet nest,
A quaint, old ring—inside engraved: "From Frank."
    Now grandpa's name
Was James, for generations it has been just the same.
It seems so strange that grandmama could ever have been
    young,
And wrapt up rings in lavender, or love-tunes ever sung.
It seems still queerer, when I think that *I* shall ever be
A great-great-grandmama, and folks will talk the same of
    me.
And wonder, as I wonder now, who "Frank," or
    "Harry" was,
And if they were my lovers? and all—and just because
They'll find a tiny scrap, or ring, or some old trinket,
    where
I've laid it—never reck'ning of the bright young eye
    who'll share
With me my well-kept secret, a hundred years from now,
And wonder where it came from, from whom, and when,
    and how.
And isn't it strange that *I* should be the first in all these
    years,
To find the treasured trinket, with its tale of unshed
    tears?
I'll put them back—the scraps and all—and lock the old
    chest tight,

And all my "private letters," I'll mark this very night.
"To be destroyed *unopened*"—I'll be sure before I go
My grandchild, or great-great-grandchild, shall never
    know
Their contents — then I'll rest content, that when one
    hundred years
Have rolled away, 'midst storm and shine, weighed down
    with smiles and tears,
*My* great-great-grandchild shall not muse, as I have
    mused to-day.
Why, great-great-grandpa's name was James, while
    Frank was in the way.
I've half a mind to neatly fold this lock of yellow hair—
(It is *my own*), together with this plain gold ring, that
    Clare—
My dearest friend at Madam Sharp's, but just a week
    ago,
Gave me. My great-great-grandchildren, I'm sure, will
    never know
The difference, and I guess I'll lay them both away,
And then, a hundred years from now, I wonder what
    they'll say.
"Why, here's a ring! A lock of hair! Come girls,
    come quick and look!
How delightfully romantic! It seems just like a book.

And what is *this?* 'From Clare'— that stands for
 Clarence—why, I know
That was not great-great-grandpa's name—and yet it
 must be so.
But great-great-grandpa's name was—"well, anything
 you choose;"
And then the foolish children will fly to tell the news,
How great-great-grandma was in love—had kept a lock
 of hair,
And a ring—a plain gold ring—that *Clarence* used to
 wear.
And my dry old bones will rattle, within their narrow
 bed,
With laughter, thinking how the world jogs on—instead
Of making new ideas, they cling closely to the old—
And take the false down for the true—the glitter for the
 gold.
And state as *facts* what none can prove, call wrong con-
 clusions right,
And turn the whole world upside down—turn day-light
 into night
For "History repeats itself," and it is hard to tell
That great-great-grandma has not played a trick on *me*
 as well.

That " Frank " *might* have been " Frances," a school-
    girl friend, 'tis true—
But then, the ring and lavender—*I* don't think so, do
    you?

## RETRIBUTION.

O NE week since my wedding? I know, Tom, I know
 I ought to be happy—my wife "all the go?"
Just listen, old boy, and I'll tell you it all :—
I met her the night of the Cavalry Ball.
Tall, stately—with eyes of the deepest of black ;
Fine form, pearly teeth—we were all on the rack.
An heiress to millions—and in her own right—
By Jove! I believe I was crazy that night,
When I met those dark eyes. You know, Tom, my
 boy—
Folks thought I was wealthy—and many a decoy
Was set by manœuvering mamas and gay belles—
But I baffled them all—let them think—for it tells
For a fellow—and, yet, Tom—betwixt you and me—
I was hard up. By Jove! Tom, old boy—don't you
 see
I needed a wife with a purse full of gold?
For mine was nigh empty, and, by George! they were
 sold,
Who counted my money. So you see, Tom, that night

I went in for the stakes. I know 'twas not right—
I played well my part—played the deuce, Tom, and all—
I was desperate! However, she asked me to call.
I did—and I asked at the door for " Miss Clair "—
The heiress's name—sent my card—on the stair
A light footfall, I rose, as she came in the door—
I arose, and stood rooted, old boy, to the floor.
Not Miss Clair—but, Tom, from that moment my heart
Was no more my own—and a pain, like a dart,
Shot through it. And why, Tom, I scracely can tell,
But the eyes were so pleading—old boy—that—ah, well!
And the sweet face, and changeable color, and all—
And the start of surprise. Then she asked did I call
For Miss Clair? Excuse her—she misunderstood
The maid-servant's message; she hoped that I would
Forgive the delay, and my card should, at once,
Be sent to Miss Clair. Tom, I'd stood like a dunce,
All those moments, spell-bound by the lovliest face
I ever had seen—the ineffable grace,
And innocent frankness, the pleading grey eyes,
Uplifted to mine, in their childish surprise,
Held my gaze, like a spell, and before I had found
My voice—she had gone. In a moment a sound
Of stiff rustling silk broke the spell, and Miss Clair
Stood before me, all graciousness. queenly, and fair.
But, somehow, she didn't appear quite the prize

She'd appeared on that night, to my poor, dazzled eyes.
But I knew I must play out the game. If I lost
My ruin was certain—I'd counted the cost.
"So sorry to keep you so long"—so she said,
But my card had been given to Clara, instead—
A young orphan, a penniless friend, who had come
To stay for a time at her beautiful home.
And all as a sort of apology, Tom—
For "poor Clara." And then the talk drifted on,
To others. Well, after that day, not a week
But I called at Miss Clair's. For whom did I seek?
The heiress, of course; but how often I met
Her friend, with the lovely soft eyes. Tom, it set
My very heart bounding; and sometimes when we
Were alone—when the heiress was out—or when she
Had not yet appeared, we conversed, and I found
How wide was her reading—and how clear, Tom, and
    sound
Was her reasoning. On music, art, books, Tom—and
    all—
I led her to talk, but nothing would pall
On her interest. And the sweet eyes would grow dark.
And I drank in their spell, like a fool, till no spark
Of love for the heiress remained, Tom, but I
Had ventured my all; I must win her, or die.
But when, at my coming, the color would rise,

And the sweet light of welcome would soften her eyes—
It took all my strength—my heart was so wrung,
To keep back the words that were burning my tongue.
But I did, Tom; at last, I asked for her hand—
The heiress of course—and in all the land,
They said that no luckier fellow than I
Existed—and all—how I wished I might die!
Well, I called, Tom, next day, and the innocent eyes
Met mine, in their frankness and startled surprise.
"Heard the news? What news?" No, Miss Clair had been late
Last night, and her friend grown too tired to wait
Her return. Would I tell her? The soft glance upraised,
With a blush. Then I told, with my poor brain half dazed.
No start of surprise, just a long searching glance
Of the eyes. Tom, it pierced through my heart like a lance.
That one, dreadful moment, her pure soul had read
The baseness of mine. Then she pleasantly said
She wished us much joy, and the eyes left my face;
And if aught had pained her, she showed not a trace.
But the eyes! and that glance! Shall I ever forget!
No, never! Great God, Tom, they're haunting me yet.
We were married, and the denouncement came.

I confessed to my bride, and not without shame,
My debts, Tom, and all—how I hadn't a cent;
For the ring and my gloves, the last dime had been spent.
My wife rose up, then—quite calm, but I saw
The tempest was coming.  I cared not a straw.
I was desperate, Tom, but I paled to the lips
When I learned the whole truth—took it in as by sips.
There'd been a mistake.  She hadn't a dime,
And Clara's the heiress; she had, all the time,
Been playing a part.  And Clara had urged
The use of her money—and all—she had "splurged."
So she told me—and all in the coolest of tone.
I stood there, old boy, as if turned into stone.
Well, Tom, I am ruined.  To-morrow 'twill be
Discussed 'round town.  Don't look so at me!
I'm wretched enough.  It is my fault you say?
I know it, don't taunt me, old boy, in that way!
My wife?  Well, she married for money, as well
As myself.  One can't wonder the miserable "sell"
Has turned her away.  I am sure, as for that,
She's as bad, Tom, as I am; 'twas but "tit for tat."
I could bear it, old boy, the disgrace, debts and all,
With one voice to cheer me whenever I fall.
And I'd give half my life, to live over again
Those past months, so freighted with sorrow and pain.
A curse on the money! the glittering lie!

It lures us with its promises on till we die!
A curse on the money! the root of all wrong!
I but followed along with the rest of the throng,
Who are grappling for gold, and trampling from sight,
'Neath their pitiless feet, every feeling of right.
And cursed are the wretches, who, when all is done,
Find, too late, they have lost by the game, and not won.
And remember, old boy, all our sorrows and joys
Depend on this fact; hearts are dangerous toys.
And he who would think to win peace will be sold
If he builds all his hopes on the treacherous gold.

# ·: JACK :: THORNTON'S :: MISTAKE :·

## ·:: *A Novel in Verse* ::·

## JACK THORNTON'S MISTAKE.

### A NOVEL IN VERSE.

"COME in, Ned, old boy—take a chair; on that shelf
Are cigars and a meerschaum—fill up, help yourself.
'Tis an age since you lent me the light of your smile.
Come! tell me, I pray, where you've been all the while.
Been 'courting' I hear—if report tells me true,
There'll soon be one less in our 'Bachelor Crew.'
You'll tell me the name of the lady, old boy?
We've been cronies too long for you now to be coy.
You can trust to Jack Thornton; come, tell me I say—
Quick! Out with it, Ned! without further delay."

"Well, the truth is, my friend—'tis, as yet, but a bet—
In fact, to be frank, Jack—I haven't asked yet;
But there's no use denying her dark, tender eyes
Play the deuce with my heartstrings—or, as it all lies
In a nutshell—you see, I am madly in love.
There! the murder is out. Let me tell you—above
The Park, there's a road to the right, that winds round
The mountains, and on to the sea—there I found
My fair Dulcinea—in a garden of flowers,
Replete with rude arbors and picturesque bowers.
Chancing once in my walk to stray down this same road,
I came, unsuspecting, upon this abode—
O'er grown with white roses and shy passion vine,
While over the windows bright nasturtiums twine.
And flitting about, 'mongst the flowers, a maid—
Ah, Jack, boy, words fail me—enough that it paid
Me well for my walk there—one 'wildering glance,
Half startled, half shy—how it made my heart dance!
By Jove! I had lifted my hat, 'fore I thought—
And, slight though the act, to her sweet face it brought
A blush, then she turned—and an oak tree soon hid
Her light form from view—but the meeting undid

My nerves for that day and I walked slowly home—
That was two years ago, Jack—while you were in Rome.
Well, my friend, after that, I was not to blame
I am sure, if my steps bent that way—and I claim
'Twas but natural to cast furtive glances within
That lovely inclosure.  But ne'er did I win,
Since that day, one glance from the beautiful eyes.
No—try as I might, not a look could surprise.
'Tho' I saw her quite often—but, always her face
Was hidden beneath a broad-brim—but the lace
Encircling her throat, was in sight 'neath the rim.
But Jack, even that filled my cup to the brim.
Well, it went on this way for a year—till one eve
I attended a soiree—quite grand—Mrs. Reeve
Was the hostess.  I stood near the door, beating time
To the music that floated about in sweet rhyme,
And listlessly watched the rainbow-hued throng
That poured in.  How stale it all seemed; before long
I was sated with color, and perfume, and chaff,
And the insipid smile, and the soft, made up laugh—
And had almost decided to make my adieux,
" So sorry to leave—and the pleasure to lose "—

For you see, Jack, those months had conspired to awake
A thirst that these flimsy world joys could not slake.
But, all thoughts of leaving in an instant fled far,
'Fore the vision, that burst on my gaze—as a star
Bursts through the blue vault, and enchains the rapt eye
So my vision was chained—I could scarcely help a cry
Of delight—for, my friend, to be plain—in the door
Stood my fair Dulcinea—Ask not what she wore—
But—you're laughing, old boy—ah, well, never mind
Just wait till you feel it—and *then* you will find
I have not enlarged on the truth. Well, I stayed—
But, 'tis no use rehearsing the progress I made
Suffice that I call at her home—and the end
You can guess without aid, for to-morrow I wend
My way to her side—and, if love reads aright
She will not say me nay—and 'fore this time next night,
I'll be, Jack, the happiest man in the town.
Her name, boy? By Jove! I forgot—Clara Brown."
" Great Heavens!" Ned started, and gazed in surprise
At the pallid white face, and the fierce, blazing eyes
Of his friend, as he sprung from his seat, with a bound.

"What ails you Jack Thornton? have the wild witches found
Your senses? What means that demoniac yell?"
"No less savage way would begin, Ned to tell
The depth of my sympathy—Your hand, Ned, old boy,
May your life be one season of unalloyed joy;
May your wife never handle the broom the wrong end,
Nor missels like irons or frying pans send."
Jack suddenly burst in a light teasing laugh
Echoed loudly by Ned. "Come! Enough of your chaff!
I'm off." "Luck attend! May the Fates turn the wheel
In your favor. Good night, boy—good luck in your deal!"
Jack fastened the door and returned to his chair
With a look on his face of the saddest despair.
"Oh, Clara," he murmured, "my darling—must I
Relinquish the struggle—and let all hope die?
Oh, the fool that I've been to imagine I e'er
Could win her from men Nature fashioned so fair!
Ah, Ned! with your supple young limbs and those eyes,

That can melt into tenderness, laugh, or look wise,
And that air of unconscious protection, and all,
Must have done execution, the night of the ball.
What madness to hope to be first in the race
With men like Ned Dayton! But I can not face
His light-hearted happiness—no, I must go
Away from it all, or, by Jove! well I know
I should *hate* him!" and rising he strode down the room,
Then back to his chair—the bright face agloom
With the thought that is hard for the bravest to bear
That the one the heart held as its holiest care
Has flown. And we look 'round the tenantless room,
And shrink back in dread from the silence and gloom.
Dead to me! and my best friend, Ned Dayton—Oh, Ned
There are hundreds of girls you could have in her stead.
Yet, fool that I am! were she free, would she take
My heart and hand. No! this serves to awake
My slumbering senses—we never could be
Ought dearer than *friends*—but she shall never see
How the cruel wound bleeds, for to-morrow I'm off
To the mountains—in hunting, this dead weight to doff
If I can, yes, *if*—but before, I must say

Good-bye to her—then for my grand holiday?
Let's see what's the time? Eight o'clock—not too late
To say a few words—Well, here goes! Come ye Fate!
I can baffle you now—and Clara, dear one,
Your heart shall not ache, that I am undone."
Let's view him—our hero—as standing before
The grate. It is plain to the very heart's core
He feels this new sorrow—the sword has cut deep;
The white, tightened lips show how hard 'tis to keep
Down the passion that swells in his breast like a sea
Lashed on by a hurricane. Gladly and free,
Spring up the red flames reaching out their long arms
And whispering low of the Fire Fiend's alarms
Then cower and crouch in a corner, and then
Burst into wild madness—then cower again—
Like the love, hate, defiance, and self-pity too,
That looks from his eyes—though he strives to subdue.
"Ah well! So it be! I am not the sole one
Who is bidden his own deep heart teachings to shun,"
And leaving the room, he strode down the stair,
And out through the night, till the street-lamp's dull
    glare

Grew dimmer. On still, to the flowery nest
Surrounding the home and the one beloved best.
He paused before entering the low wicket gate,
Paused a moment, to let his heart beatings abate.
Thus standing his gaze wandered slowly around
The picturesque garden—the tree—till a sound
Broke the stillness; the softened and low murmured
    hum
Of voices, low spoken, and seeming to come
From the parlor, close by—and his heart gave a leap—
"It is Clara," he murmured, "one look! I will creep
To the window, and view her bright head, bent low o'er
The book she is reading to 'Father,' before
I make known my presence—" and scaling the wall
He crept to the window and peeped in—but all
His bright pictures vanished—a dull glow o'erspread
His face slowly changing to ash gray instead.
'Neath the gas stood a lady, robed wholly in white.
Her dark eyes uplifted and bathed in the light,
Were met by two more—and the small hand was clasped
In another—Ned Dayton's! Jack breathed thick and
    fast—

And crouching, he watched with a fast beating heart
The two—then he sprang back a step with a start—
Ned Dayton had caught the eight form to his breast
And pressed his first kiss to her lips—But the rest
Jack stayed not to see, but, with long rapid strides,
Disappeared down the walk—on! on! near beside
Himself in his agony, knowing not where
His footsteps were straying—until the red glare
Of the street-lamps aroused him, and wending his way
To his room, he prepared his valise. The next day
The city was minus Jack Thornton. Folks said
He had "gone to the mountains"—and this report led
To no speculation, except by a few—
Clara Brown and Ned Dayton, of these, being two.

\*   \*   \*   \*   \*   \*

Jack wandered about for a good year and more
Trying, vainly, to drown all remembrance that bore
Such sadness for him. And one day in his room
He was smoking and musing—enwrapped in his gloom.
Could this be Jack Thornton, whose once ringing laugh
Was loudest and gayest—whose light, teasing chaff
Caused the gravest to smile? What a powerful thing

Is this love, that subdues, be it peasant or king!
While thus he was musing a tap at the door
Came soft, but it failed to arouse him; the sore
Heart had not found the relief that it sought,
And refused to obey the injunctions he taught.
Thus lost in his reverie, naught heeded he
The turn of the latch, nor as yet did he see
The tall form that softly approached him behind,
Till the words "Jack, old fellow!" made known to his
    mind
A presence. He sprang from his chair with a bound—
His eyes fiercely blazing, and teeth tightly ground
Together. Recovering himself with a start,
He offered his hand, and a chair—for his part
He must play, to defraud the cold world's cruel eye
Of the sight of his anguish. Not one broken sigh
Should it hear. "Well, old boy! too late, I suppose
For well wishes. No doubt, by this time, it all grows
Monotonous—greetings, best wishes and all,
And how is your wife? Or does that question pall
Already? "My wife is quite well, thank you Jack.
She is longing to see you—and you're to go back

On a visit, my friend.   Marie surely would make
My life a long torment—should I fail to take
You back home with me."   "Marie?  Why do you call
Her that, Ned?"   "Why, Jack, you are crazy and all?
'Tis her name—What else should I call her, my boy?
I've exhausted the lists of 'my pride' and 'my joy'—
Long since."   "But, good Heavens! her name 'fore she
     wed,
You told me was Clara—I'm sure that you said
It was.  Don't act like a fool—What's the row?
Say, what are you laughing so wildly at now?"
Jack glared at his friend, half believing his mirth
Was because he'd discovered how little was worth
All else to Jack Thornton, now Clara was gone—
And his teeth clenched, in thinking how plainly he'd
     worn
His heart on his sleeve.   "Come, Jack, boy, don't act
In that tragic way.  Don't!  I'll tell you—the fact
Of the case is:  I did ask Miss Clara, but she,
Quite foreign to all I had hoped, refused me.
Well, Jack, at the moment I thought my heart broke
And, clasping her wildly, I ravingly spoke

Rapid words of mad love, and I swore that I would
Ne'er relinquish her; for—I was stung—in the mood
For rash vows. But not six months from then at the
    Lakes
I met a most beautiful girl—Marie Drakes.
But the rest you now know, and we have been wed
For two months. Miss Clara is buried and dead
For aught that she enters *my* thoughts. Well, old man,
You'll come back with me? We'll do all that we can
To make your stay pleasant—good-bye for to-day
To-morrow we leave—Come prepared for a stay."
But the door had scarce closed on his friend ere the key
He had turned—Shot the bolt, and was down on one
    knee
'Fore his bureau and trunk, with his big valise out,
And began, in man fashion, to toss things about.
"The train leaves at four—and 'tis ten minutes walk
To the station, from here—there's no time for talk—
It is three o'clock now—There! I guess that will do.
Now my overcoat, ulster, cigars, one or two,
And now I am ready—Good-bye to the hills,

To the pines, and the woods and the murmuring rills.
Oh, Clara—dear heart! I shall see you again,
And forget, in your presence, this past year of pain.
We can never be more than just friends, that I know,
But we used to be that in the days long ago.
When you called me 'Old Jack' and teased me till I
Was forced to hit back, and at last you would cry
For 'quits'—there's the whistle. Ye hills, once again
I bid ye farewell!" and he sprang on the train.
That night found our hero once more on his way
To the cottage, and wondering what he would say
In excuse for his absence; just then shone the light
In the window, Jack leaped o'er the fence at the sight
And crept to the casement, peeped in, no one there
But Clara, intent on her book—her bright hair
Falling over the hand that supported her head
And her great eyes all dark with the words as she
    read.
Jack stealthly mounted the steps—tried the latch.
Ah, good! 'tis not fastened—and now but to catch
Miss Clara, before she has seen him—and see

Her start of surprise—then her innocent glee
To welcome the truant.  Jack opened the door,
And softly approached her, a board of the floor
Betrayed him by creaking beneath his light tread,
And Clara had lifted her sunny-crowned head.
For a moment the dark eyes grew large with affright,
And she half started up, as if ready for flight.
But, turning, she fled to his arms like a dove
Will flee to its mate.  "Jack! Jack! here above
The earth!  I thought you were dead, and — and —
 and"—
The sobs choked her voice, and unable to stand
The look in his eyes, she sank down to the floor,
With her face in her hands, and her hair falling o'er
The small, slender hand — and the sobs shook her frame
In their power, like a reed — All the while 'twas *his*
 name
She murmured.  His heart beat so wildly and loud
He could hear its mad throbbings—then tenderly bowed
His head over hers—parted back the bright veil—
The surprise, scarce believed, turned his face ashy pale,
But she sprung from the floor, with a low cry of shame,

"Oh, Jack, 'tis because you so suddenly came
Upon me. Now, truant! and where have you been!"
And she laughed, trying vainly her spirits to win
Back again—but Jack's eyes had been opened too wide
To be closed very easily. " Put that aside
For the present. I'll tell by and by, Clara dear,
Do you know why I've stayed from your side all this
    year?
To try to forget your sweet face, but—no use—
The boy with the arrows resents all abuse.
So I'm here "--But enough! Neither you would,
    nor I
Thank reporters, if into such scenes they should pry
So we draw down the curtain, and after an hour,
Feel safe in again stepping into " Love's Bower."
" But, why did you try to forget me? Say, Jack,"
She pouted—" and if so, what made you come back?"
Then he told her it all—how he thought she would
    wed
Ned Dayton. " Oh, Jack, what a stupid old head
Yours is, to be sure! Had it not been for—well
*Somebody*, you know—oh, I never shall tell?—

I might have—but—Jack, you don't half deserve
To be happy, to fly off like that—I should serve
You right, if I took back each word I have said,
And then—well, it wouldn't be *me* you would wed.
You—" but for some reason, best known to the two,
The sentence was cut off quite short at the " you."
"Oh, Clara," Jack's eyes grew round with affright,
"I must go by to-night's train, straight back—yes,
    to-night,
I've promised Ned Dayton to meet his young wife
To-morrow. By Jove! I would not for my life,
Have him know this and so I must leave in an hour
But, I'll bear it—there'll be no dark cloud now to
    lower—
I can face him—Ned Dayton—to-morrow I guess
With as glad eyes as his. But time's up! Heaven
    bless
This sweet face! Good-bye, love—One more, only *one*,
Dear heart! Come, please Clara—and then I am done.
There! I'm off to Ned Dayton. I wish he were here
To save me this journey away from you, dear."

"No cause for the journey, old boy! Thought you'd need
My presence—so followed you here with all speed."
And, in through the window a mischievous head
Crowned with dark, curling locks, thrust itself, but instead
Of relief, one would think Jack was facing his doom.
And, with one frightened look, Clara fled from the room.
"Well, Jack, boy! So *this* is the meaning of all
The months you have hidden away from our call!
You must have thought, man—I was greener than green
When I told you of Clara, not then to have seen
How dear was her name—But I chose to ignore
It all, then—when I too bowed down to adore
Your idol. Enough! it is late, we must go.
I'm off to my wife. Jack, I swear that I know
No more than a baby of aught you have said—
I had just reached the place, when I thrust in my head.
Good night, boy—I wish you all joy—may your wife
Never scold more than mine—and no happier life,

My friend can I wish you—good night—I appeal
To your own words, some time since, "Good luck in
   your deal."

www.ingramcontent.com/pod-product-compliance
Lightning Source LLC
Chambersburg PA
CBHW021948160426
43195CB00011B/1268